COMPLETE
BACH TRANSCRIPTIONS
FOR SOLO PIANO

Complete
Bach Transcriptions
for Solo Piano

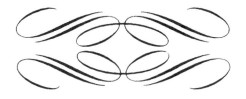

Franz Liszt

DOVER PUBLICATIONS, INC.
Mineola, New York

Copyright

Copyright © 2003 by Dover Publications, Inc.
All rights reserved.

Bibliographical Note

This Dover edition, first published in 2003, is a new compilation of works
originally published in an authoritative early edition. The list of contents and
main headings are newly added.

International Standard Book Number

ISBN-13: 978-0-486-42661-7
ISBN-10: 0-486-42661-0

Manufactured in the United States by Courier Corporation
42661005   2015
www.doverpublications.com

CONTENTS

The designation *BWV* refers to standard catalog numbers assigned to Johann Sebastian Bach's complete works; the designation *S*, to catalog numbers assigned to Franz Liszt's works by scholar Humphrey Searle. For the *Six Preludes and Fugues*, Searle places Liszt's dates of transcription at 1842–1850; for the *Fantasy and Fugue*, before 1872.

Organ-Fantasy and Fugue
in G Minor
(BWV 542 . S463)

1

Fuga

Six Organ Preludes and Fugues

Prelude and Fugue in A Minor

(BWV 543 . S462/1)

PRELUDE

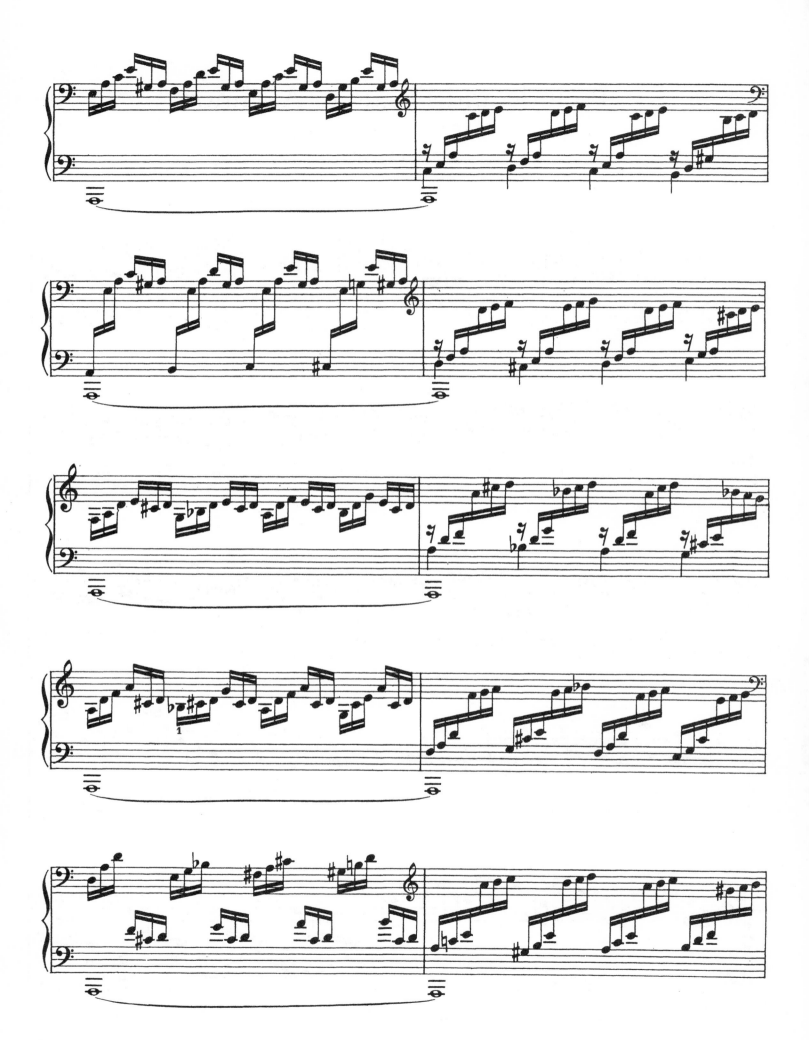

FUGUE

Prelude & Fugue in A Minor

Prelude and Fugue in C Major

(BWV 545 · S462/2)

PRELUDE

FUGUE

Allegro maestoso

Prelude & Fugue [No. 2] in C Major

Prelude and Fugue in C Minor

(BWV 546 · S462/3)

PRELUDE

FUGUE

Prelude and Fugue in C Major

(BWV 547 · S462/4)

PRELUDE

46   *Prelude & Fugue [No. 4] in C Major*

FUGUE

Prelude & Fugue [No. 4] in C Major

Prelude and Fugue in E Minor

(BWV 548 · S462/5)

PRELUDE

FUGUE

Prelude & Fugue in E Minor

Prelude & Fugue in E Minor

Prelude and Fugue in B Minor

(BWV 544 · S462/6)

PRELUDE

Prelude & Fugue in B Minor

76   *Prelude & Fugue in B Minor*

FUGUE

Prelude & Fugue in B Minor

Dover Piano and Keyboard Editions

Albeniz, Isaac, IBERIA AND ESPAÑA: Two Complete Works for Solo Piano. Spanish composer's greatest piano works in authoritative editions. Includes the popular "Tango." 192pp. 9 x 12. 0-486-25367-8

Bach, Johann Sebastian, COMPLETE KEYBOARD TRANSCRIPTIONS OF CONCERTOS BY BAROQUE COMPOSERS. Sixteen concertos by Vivaldi, Telemann and others, transcribed for solo keyboard instruments. Bach-Gesellschaft edition. 128pp. 9⅜ x 12¼. 0-486-25529-8

Bach, Johann Sebastian, COMPLETE PRELUDES AND FUGUES FOR ORGAN. All 25 of Bach's complete sets of preludes and fugues (i.e. compositions written as pairs), from the authoritative Bach-Gesellschaft edition. 168pp. 8⅜ x 11. 0-486-24816-X

Bach, Johann Sebastian, ITALIAN CONCERTO, CHROMATIC FANTASIA AND FUGUE AND OTHER WORKS FOR KEYBOARD. Sixteen of Bach's best-known, most-performed and most-recorded works for the keyboard, reproduced from the authoritative Bach-Gesellschaft edition. 112pp. 9 x 12. 0-486-25387-2

Bach, Johann Sebastian, KEYBOARD MUSIC. Bach-Gesellschaft edition. For harpsichord, piano, other keyboard instruments. English Suites, French Suites, Six Partitas, Goldberg Variations, Two-Part Inventions, Three-Part Sinfonias. 312pp. 8⅛ x 11. 0-486-22360-4

Bach, Johann Sebastian, ORGAN MUSIC. Bach-Gesellschaft edition. 93 works. 6 Trio Sonatas, German Organ Mass, Orgelbüchlein, Six Schubler Chorales, 18 Choral Preludes. 357pp. 8⅛ x 11. 0-486-22359-0

Bach, Johann Sebastian, TOCCATAS, FANTASIAS, PASSACAGLIA AND OTHER WORKS FOR ORGAN. Over 20 best-loved works including Toccata and Fugue in D Minor, BWV 565; Passacaglia and Fugue in C Minor, BWV 582, many more. Bach-Gesellschaft edition. 176pp. 9 x 12. 0-486-25403-8

Bach, Johann Sebastian, TWO- AND THREE-PART INVENTIONS. Reproduction of original autograph ms. Edited by Eric Simon. 62pp. 8⅛ x 11. 0-486-21982-8

Bach, Johann Sebastian, THE WELL-TEMPERED CLAVIER: Books I and II, Complete. All 48 preludes and fugues in all major and minor keys. Authoritative Bach-Gesellschaft edition. Explanation of ornaments in English, tempo indications, music corrections. 208pp. 9⅜ x 12¼. 0-486-24532-2

Bartók, Béla, PIANO MUSIC OF BÉLA BARTÓK, Series I. New, definitive Archive Edition incorporating composer's corrections. Includes *Funeral March* from *Kossuth, Fourteen Bagatelles,* Bartók's break to modernism. 167pp. 9 x 12. (Available in U.S. only) 0-486-24108-4

Bartók, Béla, PIANO MUSIC OF BÉLA BARTÓK, Series II. Second in the Archive Edition incorporating composer's corrections. 85 short pieces *For Children, Two Elegies, Two Romanian Dances,* etc. 192pp. 9 x 12. (Available in U.S. only) 0-486-24109-2

Beethoven, Ludwig van, BAGATELLES, RONDOS AND OTHER SHORTER WORKS FOR PIANO. Most popular and most performed shorter works, including Rondo a capriccio in G and Andante in F. Breitkopf & Härtel edition. 128pp. 9⅜ x 12¼. 0-486-25392-9

Beethoven, Ludwig van, COMPLETE PIANO SONATAS. All sonatas in fine Schenker edition, with fingering, analytical material. One of best modern editions. 615pp. 9 x 12. Two-vol. set. 0-486-23134-8, 0-486-23135-6

Beethoven, Ludwig van, COMPLETE VARIATIONS FOR SOLO PIANO, Ludwig van Beethoven. Contains all 21 sets of Beethoven's piano variations, including the extremely popular *Diabelli Variations, Op. 120.* 240pp. 9⅜ x 12¼. 0-486-25188-8

Beethoven, Ludwig van, BEETHOVEN MASTERPIECES FOR SOLO PIANO: 25 Works. Twenty-five popular pieces include the Sonata in C-sharp Minor, Op. 27, No. 2 ("Moonlight"); Sonata in D Minor, Op. 31, No. 2 ("Tempest"); 32 Variations in C Minor; Andante in F Major; Rondo Capriccio, Op. 129; Fantasia, Op. 77; and popular bagatelles, rondos, minuets, and other works. 160pp. 9 x 12. 0-486-43570-9

Blesh, Rudi (ed.), CLASSIC PIANO RAGS. Best ragtime music (1897–1922) by Scott Joplin, James Scott, Joseph F. Lamb, Tom Turpin, nine others. 364pp. 9 x 12. Introduction by Blesh. 0-486-20469-3

Brahms, Johannes, COMPLETE SHORTER WORKS FOR SOLO PIANO. All solo music not in other two volumes. Waltzes, Scherzo in E Flat Minor, Eight Pieces, Rhapsodies, Fantasies, Intermezzi, etc. Vienna Gesellschaft der Musikfreunde. 180pp. 9 x 12. 0-486-22651-4

Brahms, Johannes, COMPLETE SONATAS AND VARIATIONS FOR SOLO PIANO. All sonatas, five variations on themes from Schumann, Paganini, Handel, etc. Vienna Gesellschaft der Musikfreunde edition. 178pp. 9 x 12. 0-486-22650-6

Brahms, Johannes, COMPLETE TRANSCRIPTIONS, CADENZAS AND EXERCISES FOR SOLO PIANO. Vienna Gesellschaft der Musikfreunde edition, vol. 15. Studies after Chopin, Weber, Bach; gigues, sarabandes; 10 Hungarian dances, etc. 178pp. 9 x 12. 0-486-22652-2

Byrd, William, MY LADY NEVELLS BOOKE OF VIRGINAL MUSIC. 42 compositions in modern notation from 1591 ms. For any keyboard instrument. 245pp. 8⅛ x 11. 0-486-22246-2

Chopin, Frédéric, COMPLETE BALLADES, IMPROMPTUS AND SONATAS. The four Ballades, four Impromptus and three Sonatas. Authoritative Mikuli edition. 192pp. 9 x 12. 0-486-24164-5

Chopin, Frédéric, COMPLETE MAZURKAS, Frédéric Chopin. 51 best-loved compositions, reproduced directly from the authoritative Kistner edition edited by Carl Mikuli. 160pp. 9 x 12. 0-486-25548-4

Chopin, Frédéric, COMPLETE PRELUDES AND ETUDES FOR SOLO PIANO. All 25 Preludes and all 27 Etudes by greatest piano music composer. Authoritative Mikuli edition. 192pp. 9 x 12. 0-486-24052-5

Chopin, Frédéric, FANTASY IN F MINOR, BARCAROLLE, BERCEUSE AND OTHER WORKS FOR SOLO PIANO. 15 works, including one of the greatest of the Romantic period, the Fantasy in F Minor, Op. 49, reprinted from the authoritative German edition prepared by Chopin's student, Carl Mikuli. 224pp. 8⅜ x 11¼. 0-486-25950-1

Chopin, Frédéric, CHOPIN MASTERPIECES FOR SOLO PIANO: 46 Works. Includes Ballade No. 1 in G Minor, Berceuse, 3 ecossaises, 5 etudes, Fantaisie-Impromptu, Marche Funèbre, 8 mazurkas, 7 nocturnes, 3 polonaises, 9 preludes, Scherzo No. 2 in B-flat Minor, and 6 waltzes. Authoritative sources. 224pp. 9 x 12. 0-486-40150-2

Chopin, Frédéric, NOCTURNES AND POLONAISES. 20 *Nocturnes* and 11 *Polonaises* reproduced from the authoritative Mikuli edition for pianists, students, and musicologists. Commentary. 224pp. 9 x 12. 0-486-24564-0

Chopin, Frédéric, WALTZES AND SCHERZOS. All of the Scherzos and nearly all (20) of the Waltzes from the authoritative Mikuli edition. Editorial commentary. 160pp. 9 x 12. 0-486-24316-8

Cofone, Charles J. F. (ed.), ELIZABETH ROGERS HIR VIRGINALL BOOKE. All 112 pieces from noted 1656 manuscript, most never before published. Composers include Thomas Brewer, William Byrd, Orlando Gibbons, etc. Calligraphy by editor. 125pp. 9 x 12. 0-486-23138-0

*Available from your music dealer or write for **free** Music Catalog to*
Dover Publications, Inc., Dept. MUBI, 31 East 2nd Street, Mineola, NY 11501
*Visit us online at **www.doverpublications.com***

Dover Piano and Keyboard Editions

Couperin, François, KEYBOARD WORKS/Series One: Ordres I–XIII; Series Two: Ordres XIV–XXVII and Miscellaneous Pieces. Over 200 pieces. Reproduced directly from edition prepared by Johannes Brahms and Friedrich Chrysander. Total of 496pp. 8⅛ x 11.
Series I: 0-486-25795-9; Series II: 0-486-25796-7

Debussy, Claude, COMPLETE PRELUDES, Books 1 and 2. 24 evocative works that reveal the essence of Debussy's genius for musical imagery, among them many of the composer's most famous piano compositions. Glossary of French terms. 128pp. 8⅜ x 11¼. 0-486-25970-6

Debussy, Claude, DEBUSSY MASTERPIECES FOR SOLO PIANO: 20 Works. From France's most innovative and influential composer–a rich compilation of works that include "Golliwogg's cakewalk," "Engulfed cathedral," "Clair de lune," and 17 others. 128pp. 9 x 12. 0-486-42425-1

Debussy, Claude, PIANO MUSIC 1888–1905. Deux Arabesques, Suite Bergamesque, Masques, first series of Images, etc. Nine others, in corrected editions. 175pp. 9⅜ x 12¼. 0-486-22771-5

Dvořák, Antonín, HUMORESQUES AND OTHER WORKS FOR SOLO PIANO. Humoresques, Op. 101, complete, Silhouettes, Op. 8, Poetic Tone Pictures, Theme with Variations, Op. 36, 4 Slavonic Dances, more. 160pp. 9 x 12. 0-486-28355-0

de Falla, Manuel, AMOR BRUJO AND EL SOMBRERO DE TRES PICOS FOR SOLO PIANO. With these two popular ballets, *El Amor Brujo* (Love, the Magician) and *El Sombrero de Tres Picos* (The Three-Cornered Hat), Falla brought the world's attention to the music of Spain. The composer himself made these arrangements of the complete ballets for piano solo. xii+132pp. 9 x 12. 0-486-44170-9

Fauré, Gabriel, COMPLETE PRELUDES, IMPROMPTUS AND VALSES-CAPRICES. Eighteen elegantly wrought piano works in authoritative editions. Only one-volume collection available. 144pp. 9 x 12. (Not available in France or Germany) 0-486-25789-4

Fauré, Gabriel, NOCTURNES AND BARCAROLLES FOR SOLO PIANO. 12 nocturnes and 12 barcarolles reprinted from authoritative French editions. 208pp. 9⅜ x 12¼. (Not available in France or Germany)
0-486-27955-3

Feofanov, Dmitry (ed.), RARE MASTERPIECES OF RUSSIAN PIANO MUSIC: Eleven Pieces by Glinka, Balakirev, Glazunov and Others. Glinka's *Prayer,* Balakirev's *Reverie,* Liapunov's *Transcendental Etude, Op. 11, No. 10,* and eight others–full, authoritative scores from Russian texts. 144pp. 9 x 12. 0-486-24659-0

Franck, César, ORGAN WORKS. Composer's best-known works for organ, including Six Pieces, Trois Pieces, and Trois Chorals. Oblong format for easy use at keyboard. Authoritative Durand edition. 208pp. 11⅜ x 8¼.
0-486-25517-4

Gottschalk, Louis M., PIANO MUSIC. 26 pieces (including covers) by early 19th-century American genius. "Bamboula," "The Banjo," other Creole, Negro-based material, through elegant salon music. 301pp. 9¼ x 12.
0-486-21683-7

Granados, Enrique, GOYESCAS, SPANISH DANCES AND OTHER WORKS FOR SOLO PIANO. Great Spanish composer's most admired, most performed suites for the piano, in definitive Spanish editions. 176pp. 9 x 12.
0-486-25481-X

Grieg, Edvard, COMPLETE LYRIC PIECES FOR PIANO. All 66 pieces from Grieg's ten sets of little mood pictures for piano, favorites of generations of pianists. 224pp. 9⅜ x 12¼. 0-486-26176-X

Handel, G. F., KEYBOARD WORKS FOR SOLO INSTRUMENTS. 35 neglected works from Handel's vast oeuvre, originally jotted down as improvisations. Includes Eight Great Suites, others. New sequence. 174pp. 9⅜ x 12¼. 0-486-24338-9

Haydn, Joseph, COMPLETE PIANO SONATAS. 52 sonatas reprinted from authoritative Breitkopf & Härtel edition. Extremely clear and readable; ample space for notes, analysis. 464pp. 9⅜ x 12¼.
Vol. I: 0-486-24726-0; Vol. II: 0-486-24727-9

Jasen, David A. (ed.), RAGTIME GEMS: Original Sheet Music for 25 Ragtime Classics. Includes original sheet music and covers for 25 rags, including three of Scott Joplin's finest: "Searchlight Rag," "Rose Leaf Rag," and "Fig Leaf Rag." 122pp. 9 x 12. 0-486-25248-5

Joplin, Scott, COMPLETE PIANO RAGS. All 38 piano rags by the acknowledged master of the form, reprinted from the publisher's original editions complete with sheet music covers. Introduction by David A. Jasen. 208pp. 9 x 12. 0-486-25807-6

Liszt, Franz, ANNÉES DE PÈLERINAGE, COMPLETE. Authoritative Russian edition of piano masterpieces: *Première Année (Suisse): Deuxième Année (Italie)* and *Venezia e Napoli; Troisième Année,* other related pieces. 288pp. 9⅜ x 12¼. 0-486-25627-8

Liszt, Franz, BEETHOVEN SYMPHONIES NOS. 6–9 TRANSCRIBED FOR SOLO PIANO. Includes Symphony No. 6 in F major, Op. 68, "Pastorale"; Symphony No. 7 in A major, Op. 92; Symphony No. 8 in F major, Op. 93; and Symphony No. 9 in D minor, Op. 125, "Choral." A memorable tribute from one musical genius to another. 224pp. 9 x 12. 0-486-41884-7

Liszt, Franz, COMPLETE ETUDES FOR SOLO PIANO, Series I: Including the Transcendental Etudes, edited by Busoni. Also includes Etude in 12 Exercises, 12 Grandes Etudes and Mazeppa. Breitkopf & Härtel edition. 272pp. 8⅜ x 11¼. 0-486-25815-7

Liszt, Franz, COMPLETE ETUDES FOR SOLO PIANO, Series II: Including the Paganini Etudes and Concert Etudes, edited by Busoni. Also includes Morceau de Salon, Ab Irato. Breitkopf & Härtel edition. 192pp. 8⅜ x 11¼. 0-486-25816-5

Liszt, Franz, COMPLETE HUNGARIAN RHAPSODIES FOR SOLO PIANO. All 19 Rhapsodies reproduced directly from authoritative Russian edition. All headings, footnotes translated to English. 224pp. 8⅜ x 11¼.
0-486-24744-9

Liszt, Franz, LISZT MASTERPIECES FOR SOLO PIANO: 13 Works. Masterworks by the supreme piano virtuoso of the 19th century: *Hungarian Rhapsody No. 2 in C-sharp minor, Consolation No. 3 in D-Flat major, Liebestraum No. 3 in A-flat major, La Campanella* (Paganini Etude No. 3), and nine others. 128pp. 9 x 12. 0-486-41379-9

Liszt, Franz, MEPHISTO WALTZ AND OTHER WORKS FOR SOLO PIANO. Rapsodie Espagnole, Liebestraüme Nos. 1–3, Valse Oubliée No. 1, Nuages Gris, Polonaises Nos. 1 and 2, Grand Galop Chromatique, more. 192pp. 8⅜ x 11¼. 0-486-28147-7

Liszt, Franz, PIANO TRANSCRIPTIONS FROM FRENCH AND ITALIAN OPERAS. Virtuoso transformations of themes by Mozart, Verdi, Bellini, other masters, into unforgettable music for piano. Published in association with American Liszt Society. 247pp. 9 x 12. 0-486-24273-0

Maitland, J. Fuller, Squire, W. B. (eds.), THE FITZWILLIAM VIRGINAL BOOK. Famous early 17th-century collection of keyboard music, 300 works by Morley, Byrd, Bull, Gibbons, etc. Modern notation. Total of 938pp. 8⅜ x 11. Two-vol. set. 0-486-21068-5, 0-486-21069-3

Medtner, Nikolai, COMPLETE FAIRY TALES FOR SOLO PIANO. Thirty-eight complex, surprising pieces by an underrated Russian 20th-century Romantic whose music is more cerebral and harmonically adventurous than Rachmaninoff's. 272pp. 9 x 12. (Available in U.S. only)
0-486-41683-6

Available from your music dealer or write for ***free*** *Music Catalog to*
Dover Publications, Inc., Dept. MUBI, 31 East 2nd Street, Mineola, NY 11501
Visit us online at ***www.doverpublications.com***

Dover Piano and Keyboard Editions

Mendelssohn, Felix, COMPLETE WORKS FOR PIANOFORTE SOLO. Breitkopf and Härtel edition of Capriccio in F# Minor, Sonata in E Major, Fantasy in F# Minor, Three Caprices, Songs without Words, and 20 other works. Total of 416pp. 9⅜ x 12¼. Two-vol. set.
0-486-23136-4, 0-486-23137-2

Mozart, Wolfgang Amadeus, MOZART MASTERPIECES: 19 WORKS FOR SOLO PIANO. Superb assortment includes sonatas, fantasies, variations, rondos, minuets, and more. Highlights include "Turkish Rondo," "Sonata in C," and a dozen variations on "Ah, vous dirai-je, Maman" (the familiar tune "Twinkle, Twinkle, Little Star"). Convenient, attractive, inexpensive volume; authoritative sources. 128pp. 9 x 12.   0-486-40408-0

Pachelbel, Johann, THE FUGUES ON THE MAGNIFICAT FOR ORGAN OR KEYBOARD. 94 pieces representative of Pachelbel's magnificent contribution to keyboard composition; can be played on the organ, harpsichord or piano. 100pp. 9 x 12. (Available in U.S. only)
0-486-25037-7

Phillipp, Isidor (ed.), FRENCH PIANO MUSIC, AN ANTHOLOGY. 44 complete works, 1670–1905, by Lully, Couperin, Rameau, Alkan, Saint-Saëns, Delibes, Bizet, Godard, many others; favorite and lesser-known examples, all top quality. 188pp. 9 x 12. (Not available in France or Germany)   0-486-23381-2

Prokofiev, Sergei, PIANO SONATAS NOS. 1-4, OPP. 1, 14, 28, 29. Includes the dramatic Sonata No. 1 in F minor; Sonata No. 2 in D minor, a masterpiece in four movements; Sonata No. 3 in A minor, a brilliant 7-minute score; and Sonata No. 4 in C minor, a three-movement sonata considered vintage Prokofiev. 96pp. 9 x 12. (Available in U.S. only)   0-486-42128-7

Rachmaninoff, Serge, COMPLETE PRELUDES AND ETUDES-TABLEAUX. Forty-one of his greatest works for solo piano, including the riveting C Minor, G Minor and B Minor preludes, in authoritative editions. 208pp. 8⅜ x 11¼.   0-486-25696-0

Ravel, Maurice, PIANO MASTERPIECES OF MAURICE RAVEL. Handsome affordable treasury; *Pavane pour une infante defunte, jeux d'eau, Sonatine, Miroirs,* more. 128pp. 9 x 12. (Not available in France or Germany)   0-486-25137-3

Satie, Erik, GYMNOPÉDIES, GNOSSIENNES AND OTHER WORKS FOR PIANO. The largest Satie collection of piano works yet published, 17 in all, reprinted from the original French editions. 176pp. 9 x 12. (Not available in France or Germany)   0-486-25978-1

Satie, Erik, TWENTY SHORT PIECES FOR PIANO (Sports et Divertissements). French master's brilliant thumbnail sketches—verbal and musical—of various outdoor sports and amusements. English translations, 20 illustrations. Rare, limited 1925 edition. 48pp. 12 x 8⅞. (Not available in France or Germany)   0-486-24365-6

Scarlatti, Domenico, GREAT KEYBOARD SONATAS, Series I and Series II. 78 of the most popular sonatas reproduced from the G. Ricordi edition edited by Alessandro Longo. Total of 320pp. 8⅜ x 11¼.
Series I: 0-486-24996-4; Series II: 0-486-25003-2

Schubert, Franz, COMPLETE SONATAS FOR PIANOFORTE SOLO. All 15 sonatas. Breitkopf and Härtel edition. 293pp. 9⅜ x 12¼.
0-486-22647-6

Schubert, Franz, DANCES FOR SOLO PIANO. Over 350 waltzes, minuets, landler, ecossaises, and other charming, melodic dance compositions reprinted from the authoritative Breitkopf & Härtel edition. 192pp. 9⅜ x 12¼.
0-486-26107-7

Schubert, Franz, FIVE FAVORITE PIANO SONATAS. Here in one convenient, affordable volume are five great sonatas, including his last three, among the finest works ever composed for piano: *Sonata in C Minor, D. 958, A Major, D. 959,* and *B-flat Major, D. 960.* Also included are the sonatas in *A Minor, D. 784,* and *A Major, D. 664.* vi+122pp. 9 x 12.   0-486-44141-5

Schubert, Franz, SELECTED PIANO WORKS FOR FOUR HANDS. 24 separate pieces (16 most popular titles): Three Military Marches, Lebenssstürme, Four Polonaises, Four Ländler, etc. Rehearsal numbers added. 273pp. 9 x 12.   0-486-23529-7

Schubert, Franz, SHORTER WORKS FOR PIANOFORTE SOLO. All piano music except Sonatas, Dances, and a few unfinished pieces. Contains Wanderer, Impromptus, Moments Musicals, Variations, Scherzi, etc. Breitkopf and Härtel edition. 199pp. 9⅜ x 12¼.   0-486-22648-4

Schumann, Clara (ed.), PIANO MUSIC OF ROBERT SCHUMANN, Series I. Major compositions from the period 1830–39; *Papillons,* Toccata, Grosse Sonate No. 1, *Phantasiestücke, Arabeske, Blumenstück,* and nine other works. Reprinted from Breitkopf & Härtel edition. 274pp. 9⅜ x 12¼.
0-486-21459-1

Schumann, Clara (ed.), PIANO MUSIC OF ROBERT SCHUMANN, Series II. Major compositions from period 1838–53; *Humoreske, Novelletten,* Sonate No. 2, 43 *Clavierstücke für die Jugend,* and six other works. Reprinted from Breitkopf & Härtel edition. 272pp. 9⅜ x 12¼.   0-486-21461-3

Schumann, Clara (ed.), PIANO MUSIC OF ROBERT SCHUMANN, Series III. All solo music not in other two volumes, including *Symphonic Etudes, Phantaisie,* 13 other choice works. Definitive Breitkopf & Härtel edition. 224pp. 9⅜ x 12¼.   0-486-23906-3

Scriabin, Alexander, COMPLETE PIANO SONATAS. All ten of Scriabin's sonatas, reprinted from an authoritative early Russian edition. 256pp. 8⅜ x 11¼.   0-486-25850-5

Scriabin, Alexander, THE COMPLETE PRELUDES AND ETUDES FOR PIANOFORTE SOLO. All the preludes and etudes including many perfectly spun miniatures. Edited by K. N. Igumnov and Y. I. Mil'shteyn. 250pp. 9 x 12.   0-486-22919-X

Sousa, John Philip, SOUSA'S GREAT MARCHES IN PIANO TRANSCRIPTION. Playing edition includes: "The Stars and Stripes Forever," "King Cotton," "Washington Post," much more. 24 illustrations. 111pp. 9 x 12.   0-486-23132-1

Strauss, Johann, Jr., FAVORITE WALTZES, POLKAS AND OTHER DANCES FOR SOLO PIANO. "Blue Danube," "Tales from Vienna Woods," and many other best-known waltzes and other dances. 160pp. 9 x 12.
0-486-27851-4

Sweelinck, Jan Pieterszoon, WORKS FOR ORGAN AND KEYBOARD. Nearly all of early Dutch composer's difficult-to-find keyboard works. Chorale variations; toccatas, fantasias; variations on secular, dance tunes. Also, incomplete and/or modified works, plus fantasia by John Bull. 272pp. 9 x 12.   0-486-24935-2

Telemann, Georg Philipp, THE 36 FANTASIAS FOR KEYBOARD. Graceful compositions by 18th-century master. 1923 Breslauer edition. 80pp. 8⅛ x 11.   0-486-25365-1

Tichenor, Trebor Jay, (ed.), RAGTIME RARITIES. 63 tuneful, rediscovered piano rags by 51 composers (or teams). Does not duplicate selections in *Classic Piano Rags* (Dover, 20469-3). 305pp. 9 x 12.
0-486-23157-7

Tichenor, Trebor Jay, (ed.), RAGTIME REDISCOVERIES. 64 unusual rags demonstrate diversity of style, local tradition. Original sheet music. 320pp. 9 x 12.   0-486-23776-1

Available from your music dealer or write for free Music Catalog to
Dover Publications, Inc., Dept. MUBI, 31 East 2nd Street, Mineola, NY 11501
Visit us online at www.doverpublications.com